Unlocking Italian Citizenship

Table of Contents

The Path to Dual U.S.-Italian Citizenship for Descendants of Italian Immigrants

Unlocking Italian Citizenship

The Path to Dual U.S.-Italian Citizenship for Descendants of Italian Immigrants

Introduction

Congratulations on your decision to pursue dual U.S.-Italian citizenship by descent! This book is the result of extensive research and my own experience navigating the citizenship process. While I am not an attorney or expert, I am confident that the step-by-step guide I have provided will help you successfully understand the eligibility requirements and complete the application journey. I strongly encourage you to verify all information you read in this book to ensure the best possible outcome. With this guide, you can confidently take the first step towards acquiring your dual citizenship and enjoy all the benefits that come with it.

Unlocking Italian Citizenship

Chapter 1: Understanding Dual Citizenship

Dual citizenship, commonly known as dual nationality, is a legal status that recognizes an individual as a citizen of two countries simultaneously. In the case of dual U.S.-Italian citizenship, an individual is an official citizen of both the United States and Italy, with all the rights, privileges, and benefits that come with it. This status allows for the possession of passports from both countries, participation in the political and social life of both nations and access to a wide range of services and benefits available only to citizens. Additionally, holding an Italian passport also grants all the benefits of citizenship in the European Union, making it an extremely advantageous status for individuals seeking to broaden their horizons and enjoy the benefits of multiple citizenships.

It is important to stay well-informed with the latest updates on the requirements and guidelines provided by the Italian authorities, such as the Ministry of Interior or the Italian

Unlocking Italian Citizenship

consulate or embassy in your country. This is because the regulations and requirements may change over time. To help you get on the right track towards acquiring Italian citizenship, follow the steps mentioned in these pages. By doing so, you will be taking the necessary steps to achieve your goal. At the time of publication, following the steps below will put you on the path to Italian citizenship.

Benefits of Dual U.S.-Italian Citizenship

Freedom of Travel and Domicile: Dual citizenship provides individuals with the freedom to reside in both the United States and Europe. With a U.S. and EU passport, a dual citizen can travel, live, and work in any of the 27 EU member states, as well as in the European Economic Area (EEA) countries - including Iceland, Liechtenstein, and Norway - without the need for visas or residency permits. They can move freely between the two countries for work, study, or leisure purposes, making travel and relocation more accessible and convenient.

Enhanced Travel Privileges: Apart from unrestricted travel within the EU, an EU passport can facilitate easier travel to other countries worldwide. Many countries have visa waiver agreements or preferential treatment for EU citizens, which can result in smoother entry and shorter processing times at border checkpoints. Dual citizens can use either citizenship when applying for a travel visa.

Unlocking Italian Citizenship

Access to Healthcare and Social Services: Dual citizens have the right to access healthcare and social services provided by both the United States and any EU member state. However, it's important to note that social services are not automatically granted with citizenship. Residency and established employment in each EU member state may be required. EU residents with health insurance can and should apply for coverage under the European Health Insurance Card (EHIC) to ensure they receive necessary medical treatment during temporary stays in other EU countries. For further details, please visit the following link: https://europa.eu/youreurope/citizens/work/unemployment-and-benefits/social-security-forms/index_en.htm. Additionally, residents are eligible to access social services and benefits available to residents of other EU member states, including education, social security benefits, and other government services.

Education Benefits: EU passport holders have access to higher education institutions in EU member states under the same conditions as citizens of those countries. This includes access to universities, colleges, and vocational training programs, as well as eligibility for student loans, scholarships, and grants available to EU residents.

Employment Opportunities: Dual citizenship may open additional employment opportunities in both the United States and Europe. Holding an EU passport grants you the right to work in any EU member state without needing a work permit or visa. This opens a wide range of employment opportunities across various industries and sectors within the

 EU's single market. You can seek employment, start a business, or pursue professional opportunities in any EU country.

Cultural and Heritage Connections: Dual citizenship enables individuals to maintain strong ties to their Italian heritage and culture while also enjoying the cultural diversity and opportunities available in the United States. It allows for the preservation and celebration of family traditions, language, and customs.

Property Ownership and Inheritance Rights: Dual citizens have the same property ownership and inheritance rights as citizens of each country individually. They can own property, inherit assets, and conduct business transactions in both the United States and Italy according to the laws of each country.

Enhanced Residency and Citizenship Options: Holding an EU passport may speed up obtaining permanent residency or citizenship in an EU member state. Some countries offer accelerated residency or citizenship programs for EU citizens, providing a pathway to long-term residency or dual citizenship.

Voting Rights and Political Participation: Dual citizens have the right to participate in the political process of both the United States and Italy, including voting in elections and running for public office. They can engage in civic activities and contribute to the

Unlocking Italian Citizenship

democratic processes of both the United States and Italy. EU citizens have the right to vote and stand as candidates in local and European Parliament elections in the EU country where they reside. This provides opportunities for political engagement and participation in shaping policies and decisions at the local and EU levels.

Overall, having dual U.S.-Italian citizenship provides a unique opportunity for individuals to maintain strong connections with both countries. It also allows them to enjoy the benefits and privileges of citizenship in both nations and fosters a sense of belonging to multiple communities. Furthermore, it grants the added advantage of holding an EU passport, which opens a wealth of opportunities for travel, work, education, and lifestyle choices within the EU and beyond. Dual citizenship offers flexibility, freedom, and access to a diverse range of benefits and privileges.

Chapter 2: Eligibility Criteria

Overview of Jure Sanguinis

Italian citizenship is based on the principle of jus sanguinis (Latin: "right of blood"). This means that Italian citizenship remains intact regardless of where a child is born, as long as they were born to an Italian citizen, and as of October 3, 2024, as long as their ascendant retained citizenship while the child is still a minor. The path of Jure Sanguinis allows these true Italian citizens to claim their citizenship, by proving their unbroken line to an Italian-born ancestor within the last two generations. A line can be broken if someone in that line renounces citizenship or if the descendant is a minor when his or her father naturalizes in a jure soli country (i.e., a country that confers citizenship based on birth in that country) before 1912 (the 1912 rule), or if the only Italian-born ancestor was a woman who gave birth to the ancestor before 1948 (the 1948 rule). If a line remains unbroken, a child or grandchild in that line could be eligible to apply for Italian citizenship by descent, or jure sanguinis.

Unlocking Italian Citizenship

Criteria for Obtaining Italian Citizenship by Descent

To obtain Italian citizenship by descent individuals must meet specific criteria outlined by Italian nationality law. The eligibility criteria generally include the following:

Ancestry: The applicant must have an Italian ancestor who transferred Italian citizenship to them, either directly or through two generations. Italian citizenship can be transmitted through both the paternal and maternal lines, meaning individuals may qualify through their father's or mother's Italian citizenship.

Documentation: The applicant must provide documentation proving their lineage to the Italian ancestor from whom they are claiming citizenship. This typically includes birth certificates, marriage certificates, naturalization records (or lack thereof), and any other relevant documents demonstrating the familial relationship and Italian citizenship status of the last Italian-born ancestor.

Recognition of Citizenship

To obtain Italian citizenship by descent, applicants must submit required documentation to the appropriate Italian authorities and follow all procedures outlined by Italian nationality law. The Italian government must confirm the transmission of Italian citizenship from the last Italian-registered ancestor (LIRA) to the applicant. It is essential that neither the applicant nor any relative in the direct line to the LIRA has voluntarily renounced their Italian citizenship before applying for recognition of citizenship by descent. Renunciation of Italian citizenship may affect eligibility for citizenship by descent, and individuals who have renounced their citizenship may need to explore alternative pathways to regain Italian citizenship.

Individuals who are seeking Italian citizenship by descent should make sure to understand the specific requirements and procedures that apply to their situation. Consulting with legal experts or immigration professionals or reaching out to the nearest Italian consulate or embassy can provide valuable guidance and assistance throughout the application process.

The 1948 Rule

If you are seeking Italian citizenship by descent, it's crucial to understand the criteria and regulations involved. One such  regulation is the "1948 rule", which affects those whose Italian ancestor was born before January 1, 1948. Prior to that year, Italian law did not allow women to pass on their citizenship to their children or spouses equally, meaning that individuals with a female Italian ancestor whose child was born before 1948 may face additional challenges in proving eligibility for Italian citizenship. The 1948 rule has been the subject of legal challenges and interpretations, and there have been changes and clarifications over time. Therefore, it's prudent to consult with legal experts or specialized services familiar with navigating this aspect of Italian citizenship law to ensure that you have the most up-to-date and accurate information.

Unlocking Italian Citizenship

Rules for Naturalization of Italian Ancestors:

It is important to understand the naturalization status of your Italian ancestor to determine your eligibility for Italian citizenship by descent. Just as important is the date of the Italian ancestor's naturalization. If your Italian ancestor (parent or grandparent) became a citizen of another country before the next descendant in the line was considered an adult, the transmission of Italian citizenship may have been interrupted. However, if your Italian ancestor became a citizen of another country after the next descendant in the line became of age, then the transmission of Italian citizenship is likely to have remained intact.

Documentation proving the naturalization status of your Italian ancestor, including dates and locations, is crucial for establishing eligibility for Italian citizenship by descent. By familiarizing yourself with these additional eligibility considerations, you can better assess your qualification for Italian citizenship and navigate the application process with clarity and confidence. If your Italian ancestor lost and then re-acquired Italian citizenship while the next descendent was still a minor, then it is also possible that the line is still valid as long as they were also registered in the Anagrafe degli Italiani Residenti all'Estero (AIRE) system, or the registry of Italians residing abroad.

Unlocking Italian Citizenship

If you are trying to obtain Italian citizenship and have an ancestor who was born in Italy, you only need to find out if and when they lost their citizenship through naturalization. If they did not lose their citizenship by July 1, 1912 and you are in the paternal line, then two subsequent generations are considered Italian citizens as long as naturalization did not occur while the next descendant was a minor child. In the maternal line, two subsequent generations from January 1, 1948 are considered Italian citizens as long as her naturalization did not occur while the next descendent was a minor child. However, you must show that the citizenship was not lost before it was passed down to you. Italian citizenship can be traced back to March 17, 1861 for paternal lines and January 1st, 1948 for maternal lines.

New Ruling on October 3rd, 2024

A new court ruling has changed the way that the "rule of 1912" is interpreted for minors of Italian citizens who naturalize. This new interpretation of the law means that a child born to an Italian citizen who naturalizes in a jus soli county while they are still a minor will also lose their Italian citizenship. The definition of a minor for these purposes was considered to be under 21 years of age between July 1, 1912 and August 16th, 1992, or under 18 years of age thereafter. This loss of citizenship could only be avoided if the child is considered an emancipated minor at the time of naturalization, including if that child entered into marriage before the age of 21 (or before turning 18 if married after August 16, 1992).

Unlocking Italian Citizenship

Below are several examples of individuals who are eligible for Italian citizenship under these guidelines, including the new ruling on October 3, 2024:

1. You are born between July 1, 1912 and March 7, 1957 and your father was born in Italy or acquired Italian citizenship, registered in AIRE and remained an Italian citizen through your 21st birthday.

2. You are born after March 7, 1957 and your father was born in Italy or acquired Italian citizenship, registered in AIRE and remained an Italian citizen through your 18th birthday.

3. You are born between January 1, 1948 and March 7, 1957 and your mother was born in Italy or acquired Italian citizenship, registered in AIRE and remained an Italian citizen through your 21st birthday.

4. You are born after March 7, 1957 and your mother was born in Italy or acquired Italian citizenship, registered in AIRE and remained an Italian citizen through your 18th birthday.

5. Your father was born in the United States between July 1, 1912 and March 7, 1957 and your paternal grandfather was born in Italy or acquired Italian citizenship, registered in AIRE and remained an Italian citizen through your father's 21st birthday.

6. Your mother or father are born after and March 7, 1957 and your paternal or maternal grandfather was born in Italy or acquired Italian citizenship, registered in AIRE and remained an Italian citizen through your father or mother's 18th birthday.

7. Your mother was born between January 1, 1948 and March 7, 1957 and your maternal grandfather was born in Italy or acquired Italian citizenship, registered in AIRE and remained an Italian citizen through your mother's 21st birthday.

8. Your mother was born after March 7, 1957 and your maternal grandfather or maternal grandmother was born in Italy or acquired Italian citizenship and registered in AIRE and remained an Italian citizen through your mother's 18th birthday.

9. Your mother was born in the United States, your maternal grandfather was born in Italy or acquired Italian citizenship, registered in AIRE and remained an Italian citizen until your mother turned 21, you were born after January 1, 1948.

10. Your father was born in the United States between January 1, 1948 and March 7, 1957, your paternal grandmother was born in Italy and was an Italian citizen until your father was 21 years old.

11. Your mother was born in the United States between January 1, 1948 and March 7, 1957. Your maternal grandmother was born in Italy and was an Italian citizen until your mother's 21st birthday

Here are some references to further help you determine if you are eligible to apply:

- DIY Italian Citizenship YouTube Channel
- Italian Consulate Locations in the U.S.: https://www.italiandualcitizenship.net/italian-consulate-locations/

Unlocking Italian Citizenship

Once you have determined that you meet these eligibility requirements, the first crucial steps to put you on the path for applying for recognition of your citizenship include mapping out your family tree and gathering important dates that you will need to gather the appropriate documentation (see page 49 for a helpful chart), and a list of the documents you will need to request for each person in your line (see page 50 and 51 for a list of most requested documents). Refer to your specific consulate to determine what specific documents you will be required to submit with your application. The next few chapters and the helpful charts and checklists in the back of this book will help guide you in journey to citizenship.

Unlocking Italian Citizenship

Chapter 3: Obtaining a Thorough Family History

Researching family history and ancestry can be an exciting and rewarding journey. Here are some strategies to help you get started and in uncovering your family's past:

- **Start with What You Know:** ·Begin by gathering information about your immediate family members, including parents, grandparents, and siblings. Record names, birthdates, places of birth, marriage details and any other relevant information you know about each family member.

- **Interview Relatives:** ·Reach out to older relatives, such as parents, grandparents, aunts, uncles, and cousins, to gather oral histories and family stories. Ask about family traditions, significant events, migration patterns, occupations, and any known ancestors or relatives. significant events, migration patterns, occupations, and any known ancestors or relatives.

Unlocking Italian Citizenship

- **Document and Organize Information:** ·Keep detailed records of the information you collect, including dates, names, relationships, and sources. Use family tree software, genealogy websites, or traditional pen-and-paper methods to organize your findings and track your research progress.

- **Access Family Documents and Memorabilia:** ·Search through family documents, photos, letters, diaries, scrapbooks, and other memorabilia that may contain valuable clues about your family history. Pay attention to dates, names, locations, and any handwritten notes or annotations.

- **Utilize Online Resources:** ·Explore genealogy websites, online databases, and digital archives to access historical records, census data, birth, marriage, and death certificates, immigration records, military records, and other genealogical resources. Some popular websites for genealogical research include Ancestry.com, FamilySearch.org, MyHeritage.com, and Findmypast.com.

- **Visit Local Archives and Libraries:** Visit local libraries, historical societies, archives, and courthouses in areas where your ancestors lived to access local records, newspapers, city directories, land deeds, wills, and probate records. Librarians and archivists can provide valuable assistance and guidance in your research efforts. You might find that your library also has premium memberships with online genealogical resources such as Ancestry.com or MyHeritage.com.

Unlocking Italian Citizenship

- **Join Genealogy Societies and Forums:** Consider joining genealogy societies, forums, and online communities where you can connect with other researchers, share information, ask questions, and collaborate on research projects. Networking with fellow genealogists can provide valuable insights, tips, and support along your genealogical journey.

- **DNA Testing:** Explore the option of DNA testing through companies such as AncestryDNA, 23andMe, MyHeritageDNA, or FamilyTreeDNA. DNA testing can provide insights into your ethnic origins, genetic connections with distant relatives, and help break through brick walls in your research.

- **Verify and Cross-Check Information:** Verify the accuracy of the information you uncover by cross-checking multiple sources and records. Be critical of discrepancies, spelling variations, and conflicting information, and strive to corroborate findings through additional research and documentation.

Genealogical research often requires patience, persistence, and perseverance. Embrace the process of discovery, celebrate small victories, and be prepared for unexpected twists and turns along the way. By employing these strategies and methods, you can embark on a fulfilling journey of uncovering your family history and tracing your ancestral roots. Enjoy the adventure, and may you uncover fascinating stories and connections that enrich your understanding of your heritage.

Unlocking Italian Citizenship

Chapter 4: Italian Consulates

Locating the Nearest Italian Consulate or Embassy

The United States hosts several Italian consulates located across the country, each serving specific regions and jurisdictions. As of January 2024, here is a list of Italian consulates in the United States and the regions they serve:

1. **Consulate General of Italy in Boston, MA** - Jurisdiction: ME, MA, NH, RI, and VT. Website: https://consboston.esteri.it/en/
2. **Consulate General of Italy in Chicago, IL** - Jurisdiction: CO, IL, IA, KS, MN, MO, NE, ND, SD, WI, WY Website: https://conschicago.esteri.it/en/
3. **Consulate General of Italy in Detroit, MI** – Jurisdiction: IN, KY, MI, OH, TN Website: https://consdetroit.esteri.it/en/
4. **Consulate General of Italy in Houston, TX** - Jurisdiction: AR, LA, OK, TX Website: https://conshouston.esteri.it/en/

Unlocking Italian Citizenship

5. **Consulate General of Italy in San Francisco, CA** - Jurisdiction: Northern CA, Alaska, Guam, Hawaii, Idaho, WI, MT, Northern Nevada, OR, UT, WA, Northern Mariana Islands, Samoa, Wake Island, Midways Islands, Johnston Atoll. Website: https://conssanfrancisco.esteri.it/en/

6. **Consulate General of Italy in Los Angeles, CA** - Jurisdiction: AZ, NM, Southern CA (countiesof Imperial, Kern, Los Angeles,Orange, Riverside, San Bernardino, San Diego, San Luis Obispo,Santa Barbara, and Ventura), NV. Website: https://conslosangeles.esteri.it/en/

7. **Consulate General of Italy in Miami, FL** - Jurisdiction: AL, Cayman Islands, FL, GA, Island of Saba, MS, PR, St. Maarten, St. Eustatius, South Carolina, Turks and Caicos, and the U.S. Virgin Islands. Website: https://consmiami.esteri.it/en/

8. **Consulate Generalof Italy in New York City, New York** - Jurisdiction: NY, CT, Bermuda Islands, PA, NJ (Counties of Bergen, Essex, Hudson, Hunterdon, Mercer, Middlesex, Monmouth, Morris, Passaic, Somerset, Sussex, Union, Warren) - Website: https://consnewyork.esteri.it/en/

9. **Consulate General of Italy in Philadelphia, PA** - Jurisdiction: DE, NC, PA, WV, NJ (except forthe countiesserved by the New York consulate), MD (except for the counties of Mon Montgomery and Prince George which fall under the jurisdiction of the consular section of the Embassy), and VA (except for the counties of Arlington and Fairfax which are also under the jurisdiction of the Embassy). Website: https://consfiladelfia.esteri.it/en/

10. **Consulate General of Italy in Washington D.C** – Jurisdiction: DC, MD (Montgomery and Prince George's counties only), VA (Arlington and Fairfax counties only), city of Alexandria. Website: https://ambwashingtondc.esteri.it/en/

Unlocking Italian Citizenship

These consulates provide various services, including visa processing, passport issuance, citizenship applications, and assistance to Italian citizens residing in their respective jurisdictions.

Contact the consulate nearest to your residence or the jurisdiction that covers your area for specific inquiries and appointments. Additionally, consulate jurisdictions may change, so it's advisable to verify the latest information on their official websites or by contacting them directly.

On your appointment day, you will be given specific instructions for what type of application is required, and what consular fees are required, as well as how to submit the required documentation. You can expect that the consulate will request apostilled and translated documents for each ancestor in your Italian line, as well as their spouses. In addition, you may be required to obtain notarized signatures on your application from any living relatives in your direct line, or anyone that shares minor children with you. Pay attention to any of these details if they are present in your situation.

***Tip: Before you proceed with the next steps, check the appointment wait times for appointments at your consulate. It's not unusual to have the first available appointment at least 2 years away, and it would be a good time to get this scheduled while you work on gathering documents, getting them apostilled and translated, and filling out your application forms.**

Chapter 5: Overview of the Application Process

The application process for jure sanguinis (Italian citizenship by descent) involves several steps and varies depending on the consulate and jurisdiction. However, the typical process and processing timelines can be outlined as follows:

- **Gather Documentation:** ··Collect all necessary documentation to prove your Italian descent, including birth certificates, marriage certificates, naturalization records (or lack thereof), and other relevant documents demonstrating the lineage between you and your Italian ancestor. Certified census records are sometimes requested to determine the year of immigration for your Italian ancestor.

- **Verify Eligibility:** ·Confirm that you meet the eligibility criteria for Italian citizenship by descent, including having an ancestor within two generations who was an Italian citizen and retained Italian citizenship while their descendent was a minor child, and complying with any additional requirements imposed by Italian law.

Unlocking Italian Citizenship

- **Register for an account:** ·Create an account on the consulate website to prepare to book your citizenship appointment. Please Note: Married women should register their account under their maiden name and use their maiden name when filling out all application forms since last names don't change with marriage in Italy.

- **Schedule an Appointment:** If you have not done so already, contact the Italian consulate serving your jurisdiction to schedule an appointment for submitting your citizenship application. Appointment availability may vary, so it's advisable to schedule well in advance.

- **Final Preparation for the Citizenship Appointment:** ·Refer to the consulate website to gather any final documents, fees and required items you will need during your appointment. This may include the following: application forms which may require notarized signatures, one or two forms of government-issued identification, proof of residency, and the application fee in the form of a money order or check.

- **Submit Application and Documents:** Attend your scheduled appointment and submit your completed application form, along with all required documentation, to the consulate. Ensure that your application forms are filled out accurately and that you provide all necessary supporting documents

Unlocking Italian Citizenship

- **Pay Application Fees:** Pay any applicable application fees and charges required by the consulate or embassy. Fees may vary depending on the services requested and the consulate's fee schedule.

- **Follow-Up and Additional Documentation:** During the processing period, the consulate may request additional documentation or information to support your application. It's important to respond promptly to any requests and provide the necessary documents to expedite the processing of your application.

- **·Notification of Decision:** Once your application has been processed, you will receive notification of the consulate's decision regarding your Italian citizenship application. If approved, you will be informed of the next steps for obtaining your Italian passport and other citizenship documents.

- **·Obtain Italian Passport:** After receiving approval of your citizenship application, follow the consulate's instructions for obtaining your Italian passport and any other relevant documents. This may involve attending an appointment to submit biometric data and receiving your passport by mail or in person.

Processing timelines for jure sanguinis applications can vary significantly depending on the consulate's workload, the completeness of your application, discrepancies in documentation, and other factors. It's advisable to inquire about estimated processing times and stay informed of any updates or to the application process by contacting the consulate or embassy directly. Additionally, patience and thorough preparation are key throughout the application process for Italian citizenship by descent.

Chapter 6: Documentation Requirements

Obtaining a checklist of the necessary documentation is a crucial step in the process of applying for dual U.S.-Italian citizenship by descent. The following is a general list of required documents you will need to collect for each relative in you direct Italian line:

- ☐ Original or certified long form copy of the Italian birth record for the LIRA (no translation or apostille is required for Italian documents) that includes parent names and city of birth.

- ☐ Original or certified long-form copy of any marriage certificates connected to the direct ancestral line, including yourself. If not obtained in Italy, must also be translated into Italian and be accompanied by an apostille from the county/state where the document was issued.

- ☐ Original or certified long-form copy of birth certificates of all remaining ancestors, including yourself and your spouse and any minor child(ren). If not obtained in Italy, must also be translated into Italian and be accompanied by an apostille from the county/state where the document was issued.

- ☐ Original or certified death certificates for any ancestor in the direct Italian line or their spouse(s). If not obtained in Italy, must also be translated into Italian and be accompanied by an apostille from the county/state where the document was issued.

- ☐ Original or certified copy of naturalization certificate(s) for the Italian ancestor and their spouse, if applicable. Generally, this is the only original document that may be returned to the applicant if submitted as part of the application. US certificates of naturalization do not require translations or apostilles.

Unlocking Italian Citizenship

- [ ] Declaration of Intent/Petition for Naturalization, issued by the National Archives (www.archives.gov) for the Italian ancestor and their spouse, if applicable. Translation and apostille is not required.

- [ ] Certification of Non-Existence" (CONE) letter issued by the US Citizenship and Immigration Service (www.USCIS.gov) if no naturalization documents exist for the Italian ancestor(s). Translation and apostille is not required.

- [ ] You may be required to include divorce decrees or further documentation for any dissolved marriages or changes in guardianship along the line.

Documents issued in countries other than the United States must comply with local document authentication regulations, must be translated into Italian, and the translation must be certified by the Italian Consulate/Embassy in the country in which the documents were issued. For information on how to authenticate a document in the country of origin, you may consult the website of the competent Italian Consulate/Embassy (the list of all Italian Embassies and Consulates is available at www.esteri.it). Any discrepancies or inconsistencies must be rectified by the interested party himself through an official declaration issued by the local authorities, modifying the document to be presented in support of the application.

Unlocking Italian Citizenship

Requesting Long Form Marriage and Birth Certificates

Each state in the U.S. has a Vital Records Office responsible for maintaining birth, marriage, and death records. A long-form birth certificate will contain the full name of the parents and birthplace. A long-form marriage certificate will contain the full names of the parents for each spouse. In some cases, you may need to request both the marriage license and marriage certificate to obtain the required information instead.

You can typically request long-form certificates directly from the state's Vital Records office. Check the website of the relevant state's Vital Records Office for instructions on how to request certificates online. If you prefer to submit your request in person, you can visit the Vital Records Office or local government office in the county where the event (birth or marriage) occurred. When requesting a long-form certificate, you'll need to provide specific details such as full names, dates of birth or marriage, places of birth or marriage, and any other relevant information requested by the Vital Records Office. Keep in mind, living relatives will need to sign for their own documents, and you may be asked to provide a copy of a death certificate to request documents for any recently deceased family members. State laws may vary.

Unlocking Italian Citizenship

Obtaining an Apostille

Once you have received your documents, you will need to request an apostille for any document that was not obtained from Italy. An apostille is a certificate that authenticates the origin of a public document. Contact the Secretary of State Office in the state where the document was issued. Each Secretary of State Office has its own application process for obtaining an apostille.

This may involve submitting the original document along with a request form and payment of applicable fees. Processing times for apostilles may vary depending on the state and current workload. Be sure to inquire about processing times and any expedited services that may be available. Once the apostille is affixed to the document, it signifies that the document is authentic and can be used for legal purposes in Italy. Be sure to leave any staples or ribbons affixed once your document is authenticated. The apostille itself requires no translation and does not expire.

***Tip: Make copies of documents before submitting them for apostilles so you may work on getting the document(s) translated while you are waiting for the apostille.**

Unlocking Italian Citizenship

By following these steps, you can obtain the necessary documentation to support your application for dual U.S.-Italian citizenship by descent. It's essential to be organized, plan ahead and allow sufficient time for obtaining and processing these documents to ensure a smooth application process.

Chapter 7: Inquiring About Naturalization in the U.S.

Finding Out About the Naturalization Status of Ancestors

Here are several steps you can take to determine the naturalization status of your ancestors:

Begin with Known Information: Start by gathering any information you have about your ancestors, including their names, birthdates, birthplaces, immigration dates, and any other details related to their arrival in the United States.

- **Search Census Records:** Census records can provide valuable clues about your ancestors' immigration and naturalization status. Look for census records from 1900 onwards, as they often include information about citizenship status, year of immigration, and naturalization.

Unlocking Italian Citizenship

- ·**Explore Passenger Lists:** Search for passenger lists and immigration records documenting your ancestors' arrival in the United States. These records may provide details about their country of origin, port of departure, ship name, and immigration date, which can help narrow down the timeline for naturalization.

Check Naturalization Records: Naturalization records are key documents for determining the naturalization status of your ancestors. You can access naturalization records through various sources, including:

- **U.S. Citizenship and Immigration Services (USCIS):** USCIS provides access to naturalization records starting from 1906 through its Genealogy Program. You can submit a request for genealogical records, including naturalization files, through their website. An index search will give you the Certification File (C-File) number, which you will need to provide when requesting the Naturalization Records. A certified copy of the Petition for Naturalization and Oath of Allegiance is sufficient documentation for most consulates to show naturalization status and naturalization dates relative to the birth of your next ancestor.

Unlocking Italian Citizenship

- **National Archives and Records Administration (NARA):** NARA holds a vast collection of naturalization records, including petitions, declarations of intention, and certificates of naturalization. You can search their online catalog and request records relevant to your ancestors.

- **Local Courts and Archives:** Naturalization records were often filed in local courts where the naturalization process took place. Contact local courthouses, archives, and historical societies in the area where your ancestors lived to inquire about access to naturalization records.

- ·**Online Databases:** Explore online genealogy websites, such as Ancestry.com, FamilySearch.org, and MyHeritage.com, which may contain digitized naturalization records and indexes. These databases allow you to search for naturalization records by name, location, and other criteria.

Once you locate naturalization records for your ancestors, pay close attention to the dates listed on the documents. These dates can help determine when your ancestors became U.S. citizens. Ensure the naturalization date does not occur prior to the birth of the next-in-line ancestor (or if the next-in-line was a minor, ensure they were born after 1912).

Unlocking Italian Citizenship

If you encounter challenges locating naturalization records for your ancestors, consider exploring alternative sources of information, such as military records, passport applications, obituaries, and family correspondence, which may contain references to citizenship status.

By following these steps and conducting thorough research, you can uncover valuable information about the naturalization status of your ancestors and gain insights into their immigration journey and citizenship history.

Chapter 8: Family Members of the New Italian Citizen

Immediate Family Members

After an individual obtains Italian citizenship via jure sanguinis, their spouse and minor children may be eligible to apply for Italian citizenship through a simplified process known as "derivative citizenship" and "citizenship by marriage". Individuals considering derivative citizenship for their spouse and minor children should consult the Italian consulate or embassy serving their jurisdiction for the most accurate and up-to-date information for their specific circumstances. Here are the general steps and considerations for the spouse and minor children:

Spouse: In marriages that occurred before April 27, 1983, a spouse automatically acquired the right to Italian citizenship. The spouse would be eligible to immediately submit documentation for citizenship. For marriages occurring after April 27, 1983 outside of Italy, the spouse of an Italian citizen may be eligible to apply for Italian citizenship after being married for 3 years. The marriage must be recognized by Italian law. This is shortened to 18 cmonths if they have minor children. The waiting period is shorter if the couple resides within Italy.

Language and Integration Requirements: Spouses applying for Italian citizenship may need to meet language proficiency and integration requirements. Some consulates may require proof of knowledge of the Italian language, while others may waive this requirement.

Minor Children: Minor children (under 18 years old) of an Italian citizen who obtained citizenship through jure sanguinis can usually acquire Italian citizenship automatically through the principle of jure sanguinis. The process typically involves submitting the necessary documentation to the Italian consulate or embassy where the citizenship application will be processed. Documentation may include identification, birth certificates, marriage certificates, and other relevant guardianship documents.

Application Process: Contact the Italian consulate or embassy serving your jurisdiction to inquire about the specific requirements and application process for derivative citizenship for the spouse and minor children. Each consulate may have slightly different procedures. Complete the application forms provided by the consulate or embassy and ensure that all required documents are submitted accurately.

Unlocking Italian Citizenship

Waiting Period and Processing Time: Citizenship applications for spouses and minor children typically have a waiting period, and processing times can vary. Be prepared to wait for the consulate or embassy to review and process the applications.

Siblings Who Share a Common Italian Ancestor

In general, one sibling cannot directly use another sibling's application information to apply for Italian citizenship by descent. Italian citizenship by descent is based on a direct lineage connection to an Italian parent or grandparent. All individuals must independently prove their eligibility for Italian citizenship based on their own familial relationship to the Italian ancestor. However, there are scenarios where siblings may have overlapping eligibility for Italian citizenship based on the same lineage.

Common Ancestor: If siblings share the same Italian ancestor (e.g., the same Italian grandparent), each sibling can independently apply for Italian citizenship by descent using their own documentation and information. They would need to provide evidence of the familial relationship to the Italian ancestor through birth, marriage, and other relevant records.

Shared Documentation: Siblings may be able to share certain documentation and information related to their shared ancestry, such as birth certificates of common

Unlocking Italian Citizenship

ancestors, marriage certificates, and other relevant records. However, each sibling would still need to submit their own application and provide any additional documentation specific to their individual circumstances. Likely, this is only possible when both siblings reside in the same consular jurisdiction. Consult the appropriate consulate for instructions when one sibling wishes to reference the other sibling's application for the shared documentation.

Consultation and Assistance: Siblings can collaborate and support each other in gathering documentation, conducting research, and navigating the application process for Italian citizenship. They can share knowledge, resources, and experiences to streamline the process and address any challenges that may arise.

Professional Guidance: It's advisable for siblings to seek guidance from legal professionals or immigration experts specializing in Italian citizenship and nationality law. These professionals can provide personalized advice, assess individual eligibility, and assist with the preparation and submission of citizenship applications based on each sibling's unique circumstances.

Ultimately, each sibling must independently demonstrate their eligibility for Italian citizenship by descent based on their own lineage and familial relationship to the Italian ancestor. While siblings can collaborate and support each other throughout the application process, they cannot directly use another sibling's application information to apply for Italian citizenship.

Unlocking Italian Citizenship

Extended Family Members:

Extended family members of an individual who obtains Italian citizenship via jure sanguinis (by descent) typically cannot directly apply for Italian citizenship using the applicant's information. Italian citizenship by descent is based on a direct lineage connection to an Italian ancestor, and the right to citizenship is derived from the ancestral line rather than through extended family members. However, there are some scenarios where extended family members may indirectly benefit from a relative obtaining Italian citizenship:

Chain Migration: Once an individual obtains Italian citizenship, they may be able to sponsor certain family members for immigration to Italy under family reunification provisions. This process allows immediate family members, such as spouses, minor children, and dependent parents, to join the Italian citizen in Italy and eventually pursue their own pathways to citizenship.

Residency Rights: Extended family members who wish to reside in Italy may be eligible to apply for residence permits or visas based on family ties to an Italian citizen. These permits may allow family members to live and work in Italy legally, although they do not confer Italian citizenship directly.

Unlocking Italian Citizenship

Future Generations: Italian citizenship acquired by descent can be passed down through future generations, allowing descendants of an Italian citizen to claim citizenship in subsequent generations. However, each generation must meet the eligibility criteria and follow the appropriate application process to assert their right to Italian citizenship. For children born after you receive Italian citizenship, you must register their births prior to their turning 18 for their Italian citizenship to be recognized. To register a birth certificate through an Italian consulate, you must fill out and mail a form to the consulate covering your residential jurisdiction with their Italian-translated and Apostilled birth certificate.

Specific requirements and processes may vary depending on the jurisdiction and consulate or embassy where the application is submitted. It's always advisable to seek guidance from the relevant authorities for the most accurate and up-to-date information tailored to one's specific circumstances. Individuals considering Italian citizenship for their family members should consult with legal professionals or immigration experts familiar with Italian nationality law and regulations. They can provide guidance on eligibility requirements, application procedures, and potential pathways to citizenship for extended family members based on individual circumstances and family history.

Unlocking Italian Citizenship

Chapter 9: Waiting Period and Application Processing

Understanding Average Processing Times for Citizenship Applications

The waiting period after submitting an application for Italian citizenship by descent can vary significantly depending on various factors, including the workload and processing times of the Italian consulate or embassy where the application was submitted, the completeness of the application, and any additional documentation or information required by the authorities. While it's challenging to provide an exact timeframe due to these variables, applicants should generally expect the following timelines:

Initial Review: Upon submission of the application, the consulate or embassy will conduct an initial review to ensure that the application is complete and meets the eligibility criteria for Italian citizenship by descent. This review may take several weeks to a few months, depending on the consulate's workload and processing times.

Unlocking Italian Citizenship

Processing Time: Once the application passes the initial review stage, it will undergo further processing, which may involve verifying the authenticity of submitted documents, conducting background checks, and assessing the applicant's eligibility for citizenship. Processing times can vary widely and may range from several months to over a year, depending on the complexity of the case and the consulate's capacity.

Additional Documentation Requests: In some cases, the consulate or embassy may request additional documentation or information to support the application. Applicants should respond promptly to these requests to avoid delays in the processing of their application. Communication and Updates: Throughout the waiting period, applicants may receive periodic updates or requests for information from the consulate or embassy. It's essential to monitor communication channels, including email, phone, and postal mail, and respond promptly to any inquiries or requests for clarification.

Final Decision: Once the application has been thoroughly reviewed and all necessary documentation has been provided, the consulate or embassy will make a final decision regarding the applicant's eligibility for Italian citizenship by descent. Applicants will receive notification of the decision, which may include approval, denial, or requests for additional information.

Unlocking Italian Citizenship

Overall, applicants should be prepared for the possibility of an extended waiting period during the application process for Italian citizenship by descent. It's advisable to remain patient, stay informed of any updates or developments, and maintain open communication with the consulate or embassy handling the application. Applicants can also seek guidance from legal professionals or immigration experts to navigate the process effectively and address any concerns or challenges that may arise.

Chapter 10: Receiving Citizenship Recognition

Registering Minor Children and Obtaining Your Italian Passport

Once you receive confirmation of your Italian citizenship, you will be registered in the Anagrafe degli Italiani Residenti all'Estero (AIRE) system, or the registry of Italians Residing Abroad. Depending on your consulate, you may also be allowed to mail in the certified, translated and apostilled copies of your marriage certificate and minor children's birth certificates to obtain Italian citizenship for your minor children. Once you are successfully registered in AIRE, you can schedule your appointment to obtain your Italian passport!

At your passport appointment, bring your US passport, passport application, application fee, and appropriately sized passport photos (if not taken on-site). Married women will use their

Unlocking Italian Citizenship

maiden name on their application but may add their married last name to page 4 of the Italian passport, which helps when booking flights with their Italian passport. The completed passport may be given at the time of the appointment or may be mailed to you.

Once your passport is received, you are probably ready to celebrate with a trip to Italy!

Unlocking Italian Citizenship

Chapter 11: Post-Citizenship Considerations

Traveling With Dual Citizenship and Passport Considerations

As a general rule of thumb, you should present the passport that matches the country you are standing in. When booking flights, enter the passport that matches where you are traveling to. You should never show both passports to immigration authorities unless specifically asked for them. There are some specific situations where it would be more advantageous to use one passport over another, such as the examples below:

- ·Some countries also offer visa-free entry to Italian citizens where they might charge a fee to Americans (example: Thailand).

- ·China is piloting 15-day visa free access for citizens of Italy, Germany, Spain, Netherlands, and Malta through November 2024.

Unlocking Italian Citizenship

- ·If your flight will connect to Europe via Canada (i.e. Toronto, Ottawa, Quebec, etc.), you should use your US passport to avoid having to get an eTA (electronic travel authorization) to Canada on your Italian passport.

- ·When you buy an international ticket from an airline, it is that airline's responsibility to ensure that you are legally able to enter the destination you are purchasing a ticket to. For this reason, you should purchase tickets to European Union, EEA, and Schengen Zone countries using the information from your Italian passport.

- ·Finally, Italy requires its own citizens to enter Italy on their Italian passports, and Italian citizens are required to carry government identification at all times. For this reason, you should get used to carrying your Italian passport whenever you are in Italy

Understanding Tax Obligations in Both Countries

Given the complexity of tax laws and regulations in both the United States and Italy, dual citizens should consider seeking advice from tax professionals who are knowledgeable about international tax matters to ensure compliance with the laws of both countries and to optimize their tax situation.

Unlocking Italian Citizenship

The United States taxes its citizens on their worldwide income, regardless of where they reside. This means that U.S. citizens, including dual citizens, are required to report their income from all sources, both within and outside the United States. Italy also taxes its residents on their worldwide income, so if a U.S.-Italian dual citizen is also a resident of Italy, they are also subject to Italian taxation on their global income. However, the tax treaty between the United States and Italy helps prevent double taxation and addresses various tax issues. Dual citizens should review the provisions of the tax treaty to understand how it affects their tax situation, including rules regarding residency, taxation of specific types of income, and tax credits or deductions available to them.

Conclusion:

Obtaining dual U.S.-Italian citizenship by descent is a journey that reconnects individuals with their Italian heritage while providing access to benefits and privileges in both countries and in the European Union. By following the steps outlined in this guide and being diligent in your preparations, you can successfully navigate the application process and realize your dream of dual citizenship. dream of dual citizenship.

Buona fortuna! (Good luck!)

Unlocking Italian Citizenship

✦✦ TO DO LIST ✦✦

- ☐ Complete Family Tree starting from your LIRA to yourself (spouse/children)
- ☐ Review citizenship application requirements on Consulate website
- ☐ Create account on Consulate website (see p. 19)
- ☐ Make Citizenship appointment (allow time to gather all documents)
- ☐ Obtain all required documents (see document checklist, next page)
- ☐ Obtain translations for all marriage, death, and birth documents not from Italy
- ☐ Obtain apostilles for all marriage, death, and birth documents not from Italy
- ☐ Request C-File from USCIS for LIRA
- ☐ Request Naturalization Records (if found) from USCIS for LIRA
- ☐ Request Naturalization Records (if needed) from NARA for LIRA
- ☐ Request Certification of Non-Existance (CONE) if no naturalization records exist
- ☐ Request certified copy of the 1st census after the birth of the 1st U.S.-born ascendant
- ☐ Complete application forms (may need notarized signatures)
- ☐ Within 1-2 months of appointment, obtain money order for correct consular fee
- ☐ Make copies of your identification card and passport to include with application
- ☐ Make a copy of recent utility bill to include in application (for proof of residence)
- ☐ Confirm appointment (if applicable)
- ☐ Organize documents, translations, application, payment, proof of residence for appt
- ☐ Smile, you are almost there!

Record your relevant family tree details and important dates and places here:

YOUR GRANDPARENTS

MATERNAL GRANDPARENTS (your mother's side)		PATERNAL GRANDPARENTS (your father's side)	
GRANDMOTHER	**GRANDFATHER**	**GRANDMOTHER**	**GRANDFATHER**
FULL NAME (+ maiden)	FULL NAME	FULL NAME (+ maiden)	FULL NAME
Birth (+date & place)	**Birth** (+date & place)	**Birth** (+date & place)	**Birth** (+date & place)
Death (+date & place)	**Death** (+date & place)	**Death** (+date & place)	**Death** (+date & place)
Naturalization (+date & place)	**Naturalization** (+date & place)	**Naturalization** (+date & place)	**Naturalization** (+date & place)
Immigration (+date & place)	**Immigration** (+date & place)	**Immigration** (+date & place)	**Immigration** (+date & place)
Marriage (+date & place)		**Marriage** (+date & place)	

YOUR PARENTS

MOTHER		FATHER	
FULL NAME (+ maiden)		FULL NAME	
Birth (+date & place)		Birth (+date & place)	
Naturalization (+date & place)	Immigration (+date & place)	Naturalization (+date & place)	Immigration (+date & place)
Marriage (+date & place)			

YOUR DETAILS

YOUR FULL NAME (as in your current PASSPORT):	
YOUR FULL NAME at BIRTH (as on your BIRTH CERTIFICATE)	

Place of birth	Date of birth	Marital status	Date of marriage 1	Place of marriage 1	Date of divorce 1	Date of marriage 2	Place of marriage 2
			if applicable	if applicable	if applicable	if applicable	if applicable

YOUR CHILDREN

FULL NAME:		FULL NAME:		FULL NAME:		FULL NAME:	
Date of birth:		Date of birth:		Date of birth:		Date of birth:	

YOUR SIBLINGS

FULL NAME:		FULL NAME:		FULL NAME:		FULL NAME:	
Date of birth:		Date of birth:		Date of birth:		Date of birth:	
Marital status:		Marital status:		Marital status:		Marital status:	

Unlocking Italian Citizenship

DOCUMENT CHECKLIST

- ☐ Certified long form copy of the Italian birth record for the LIRA
- ☐ Certified long form copy of marriage record(s) for the LIRA (if applicable)
- ☐ Certified long form copy of birth record for the LIRA's spouse (if applicable)
- ☐ Certified death record for the LIRA (if applicable)
- ☐ Certified long form copy of birth record(s) for remaining ascendant(s) and spouse(s)
- ☐ Certified long form copy of marriage record(s) for all ascendant(s)
- ☐ Certified death certificate for all ascendants, if applicable
- ☐ Certified long form copy of your birth certificate (and spouse/children, if applicable)
- ☐ Translations and apostilles of all above records not from Italy
- ☐ Apostilles for all birth and marriage records not obtained from Italy
- ☐ C-File from USCIS for LIRA
- ☐ USCIS Naturalization Record for LIRA
- ☐ NARA Naturalization Records (if needed) for LIRA
- ☐ Certification of Non-Existance (CONE) Letter if no naturalization records exist
- ☐ Certified copy of the 1st census after the birth of the 1st U.S.-born ascendant
- ☐ Any applicable divorce records (with translation and apostille)
- ☐
- ☐
- ☐

Track your important document details and dates here:

Name	Document	State/County of Issue	Date requested	Date receieved	Date Apostilled	Date Translated
LIRA:	Birth Certificate				n/a	n/a
	Death Certificate					
	USCIS Naturalization C-File				n/a	n/a
	NARA Naturalization Records				n/a	n/a
					n/a	n/a
LIRA:	Marriage Certificate				unless obtained from Italy	unless obtained from Italy
Spouse of LIRA	Birth Certificate				unless obtained from Italy	unless obtained from Italy
	Death Certificate				unless obtained from Italy	unless obtained from Italy
2nd in Line:	Birth Certificate					
	Certified Census (after birth)				n/a	n/a
	Death Certificate					
2nd in Line:	Marriage Certificate					
2nd in Line (spouse)	Birth Certificate					
	Death Certificate					
Self:	Birth Certificate					
Self (if applicable):	Marriage Certificate					
Spouse (if applicable):	Birth Certificate					
Child (if applicable):	Birth Certificate					
Child (if applicable):	Birth Certificate					
Application Form - applicant:					notarized (if applicable)	n/a

In addition to above documents, bring:
Passport
Driver's license
proof of permanent address (utility bill)
*copy of driver's license and passport
money order/certified check/cashiers check to Italian Consulate General with application fee

Unlocking Italian Citizenship

PROGRESS TRACKER

DATE	ACCOMPLISHMENT

NOTES

Unlocking Italian Citizenship

FINANCIAL TRACKER

EXPENSES		
DATE	DESCRIPTION	AMOUNT
	Total:	

NOTES

Unlocking Italian Citizenship

✦✦ TO DO LIST ✦✦

- [ ]
- [ ]
- [ ]
- [ ]
- [ ]
- [ ]
- [ ]
- [ ]
- [ ]
- [ ]
- [ ]
- [ ]
- [ ]
- [ ]
- [ ]
- [ ]
- [ ]

Unlocking Italian Citizenship

✦ ✦ TO DO LIST ✦ ✦

Unlocking Italian Citizenship

NOTES

Unlocking Italian Citizenship

NOTES

Unlocking Italian Citizenship

Memories from
My Citizenship Journey

The person who
made it all possible!

NAME/RELATION _______________________

BIRTHDATE/BIRTHPLACE _______________________

DATE OF ARRIVAL IN U.S. _______________________

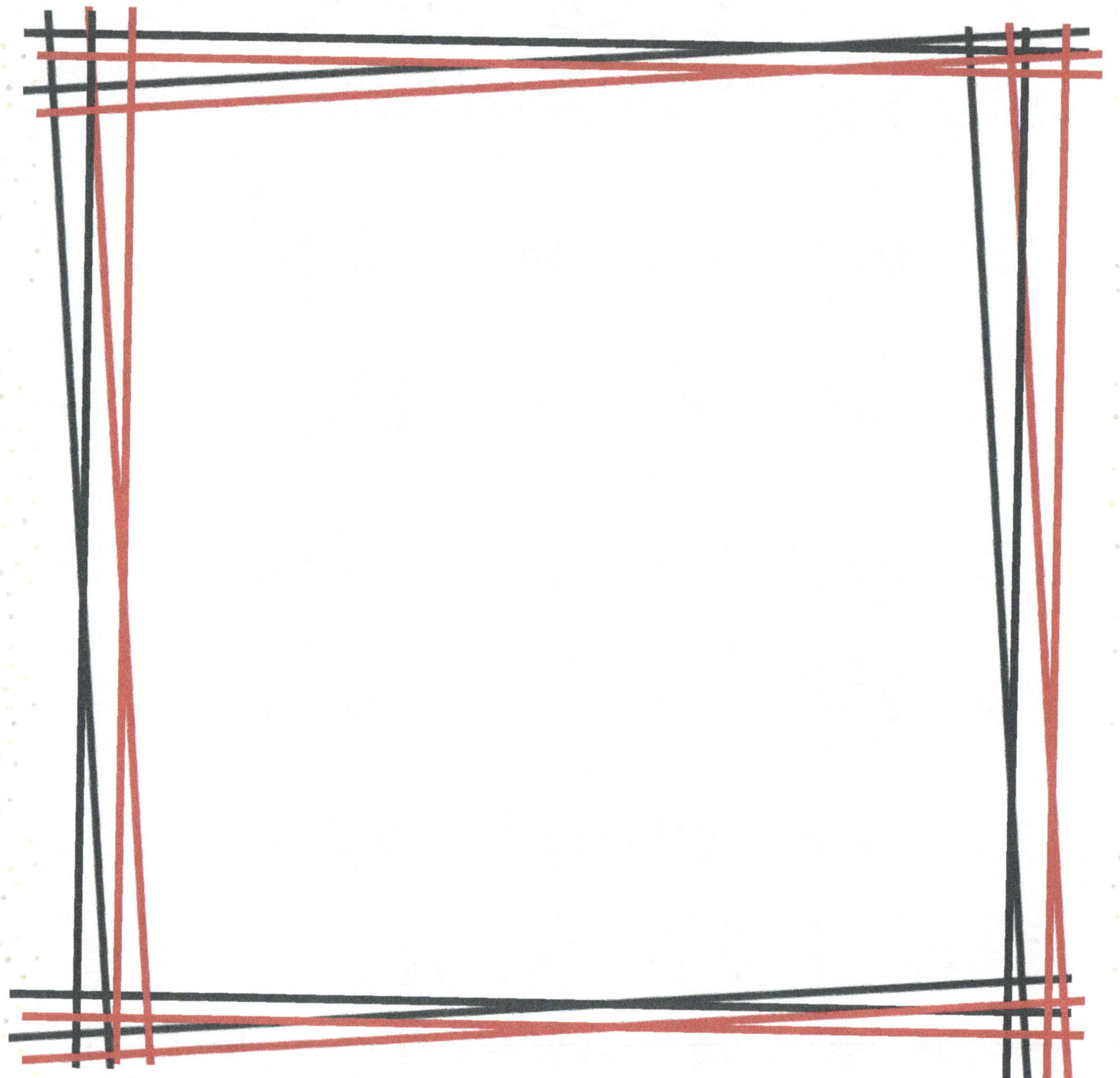

The Italian
Birth Record

The Journey to the U.S.

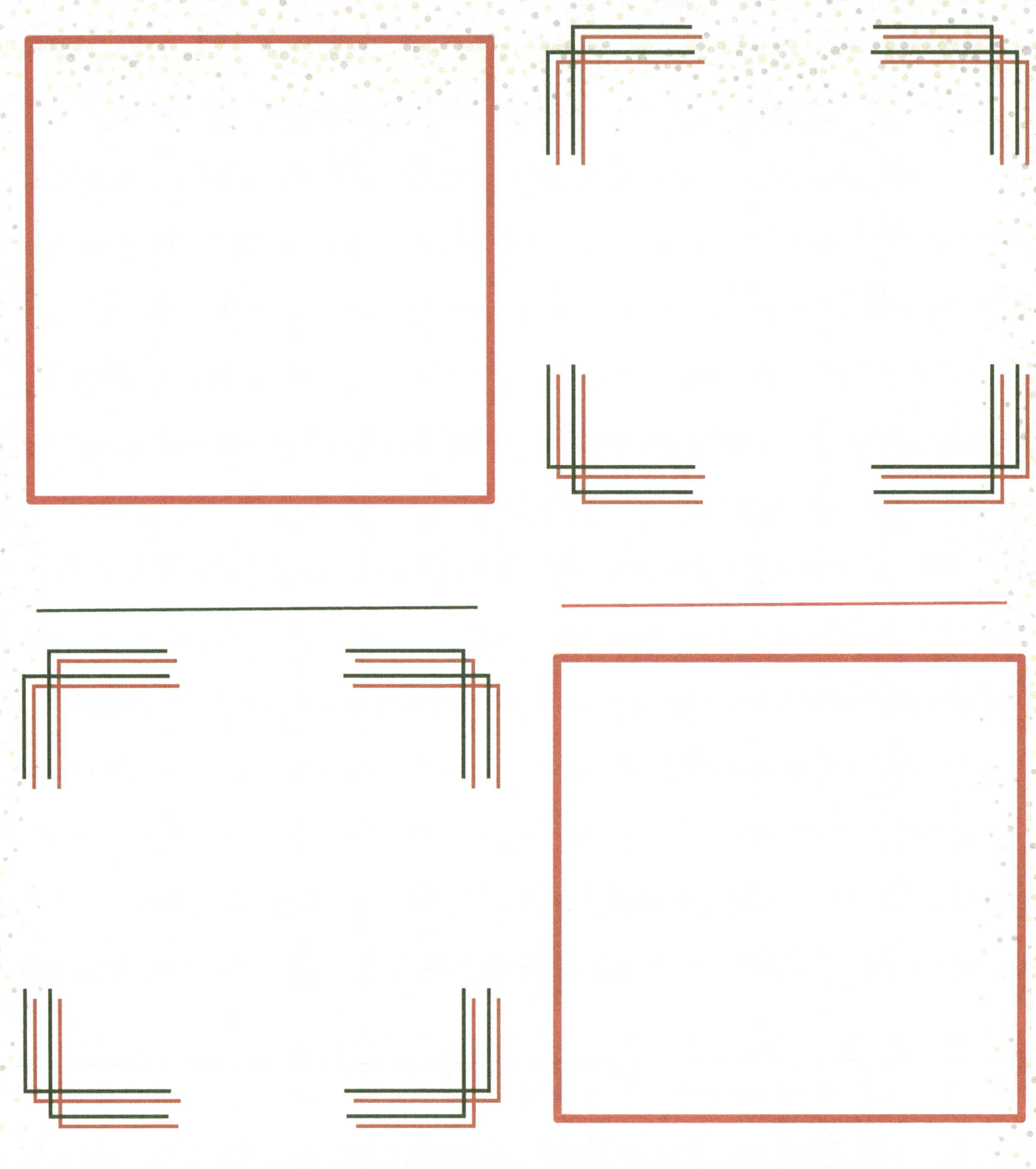

My Italian Family

Document Gathering

Appointment
Day

My Italian Passport!

Memories from the Journey

Memories from the Journey

Memories from the Journey

Memories from the Journey

Memories from the Journey

Memories from the Journey

Memories from the Journey

Unlocking Italian Citizenship

SUCCESS!

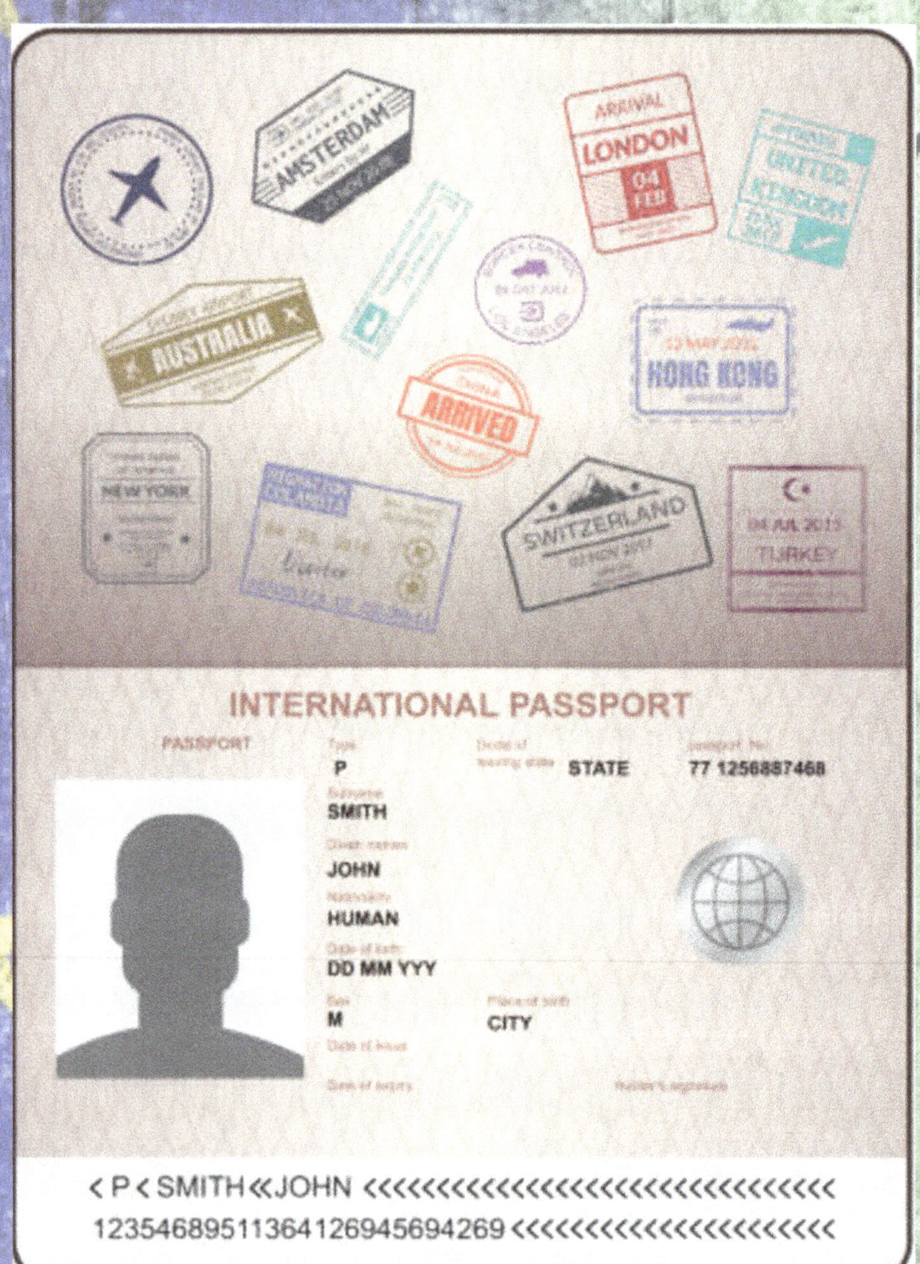

The Path to Dual U.S.-Italian Citizenship for Descendants of Italian Immigrants